An Overview of Psychological Operations (PSYOP)

Federal Research Division Library of Congress

NIMBLE BOOKS LLC: THE AI LAB FOR BOOK-LOVERS

~ FRED ZIMMERMAN, EDITOR ~

Humans and AI making books richer, more diverse, and more surprising.

Publishing Information

ISBN: 978-1-60888-302-8

AI-Generated Keyword Phrases

Psychological operations; United States; Soviet Union; Department of the Army; United States Congress; 97th; United States Information Agency;

Publisher's Notes

This annotated edition illustrates the capabilities of the AI Lab for Book-Lovers to add context and ease-of-use to manuscripts. It includes several types of abstracts, building from simplest to more complex: TLDR (one word), ELI5, TLDR (vanilla), Scientific Style, and Action Items; essays to increase viewpoint diversity, such as Grounds for Dissent, Red Team Critique, and MAGA Perspective; and Notable Passages and Nutshell Summaries for each page.

ANNOTATIONS

AI-Generated Foreword

This document provides a comprehensive overview of psychological operations (PSYOP) with a specific focus on military applications in the context of the Cold War era (up to November 1989).

Key Points:

- Definition of PSYOP: The document clarifies the evolving definition of PSYOP, from influencing enemy attitudes in wartime to a broader scope encompassing peacetime activities aimed at shaping emotions, attitudes, and behaviors of foreign groups to achieve political and military objectives.
- Historical Context: The paper explores historical examples of PSYOP, highlighting instances like Judith and Holofernes, Ghengis Khan, and the American Revolution, showcasing the enduring value of psychological tactics in warfare.
- Soviet PSYOP: The document delves into the Soviet Union's extensive and sophisticated PSYOP machinery, emphasizing their philosophy of constant ideological warfare against the capitalist world. It details the roles of various Soviet agencies like the International Department, Propaganda Department, and the KGB in conducting active measures and disinformation campaigns.
- United States PSYOP: The paper examines the US approach to PSYOP, characterized by a historical reluctance towards peacetime PSYOP and a reactive posture. It discusses the challenges faced by the US in countering Soviet propaganda and the need for improved coordination and resources.
- Evolving Landscape: The document acknowledges the changing nature of warfare, with the rise of unconventional conflicts and low-intensity conflicts, necessitating a greater emphasis on PSYOP.

Strengths of the Document:

- Comprehensive Overview: The paper provides a well-structured and informative analysis of PSYOP, covering historical examples, theoretical frameworks, and contemporary applications.
- Comparative Approach: The document effectively compares and contrasts the Soviet and US approaches to PSYOP, highlighting their strengths and weaknesses.
- Emphasis on Contemporary Challenges: The paper acknowledges the changing nature of warfare and the increasing importance of PSYOP in the context of unconventional and low-intensity conflicts.
- Potential Limitations:
- Dated Information: As the document predates November 1989, it does not consider the significant geopolitical shifts that occurred after the Cold War, such as the collapse of the Soviet Union and the rise of new threats and challenges.
- Focus on Military Applications: While the document acknowledges the broader scope of PSYOP, its primary focus remains on military applications, potentially overlooking the growing importance of PSYOP in non-military domains like diplomacy, business, and social movements.

Overall, this document offers valuable insights into the theory and practice of PSYOP during the Cold War era. However, it is crucial to consider the limitations of its dated information and recognize the evolving nature of PSYOP in the contemporary world.

Fred Zimmerman using Google Gemini 1.5

Abstracts

TL;DR (one word)

Information.

Explain It To Me Like I'm Five Years Old

Psychological operations are when one country tries to influence the thoughts and feelings of people in another country. The United States and the Soviet Union both used psychological operations to try to make people think a certain way. The United States Congress and other government agencies were involved in making decisions about these operations.

TL;DR (vanilla)

The United States and Soviet Union both engaged in psychological operations during the Cold War, as documented by various government reports and agencies.

Scientific Style

This study examines the use of psychological operations by the United States and the Soviet Union, as documented in various government publications. The Department of the Army report from 1976 provides insight into the strategies employed by both countries, while the United States Congress reports offer further analysis of the impact and effectiveness of these operations. The United States Information Agency is also cited as a key player in shaping public perception through psychological operations. This comprehensive review highlights the importance of understanding the role of psychological operations in international relations and the influence they have on shaping public opinion.

Action Items

Review the Department of the Army's publication on psychological operations for more information on the topic.

Look into the actions and policies of the United States Congress regarding psychological operations.

Consider the role of the United States Information Agency in psychological operations.

Further research the relationship between the United States and the Soviet Union in terms of psychological operations.

Viewpoints

These perspectives increase the reader's exposure to viewpoint diversity.

Grounds for Dissent

A member of the organization responsible for this document may have principled, substantive reasons to dissent from this report for several reasons.

Firstly, they may believe that the information presented in the report is biased or inaccurate. They may have access to different sources of information or data that contradict the findings of the report, leading them to question its validity.

Secondly, they may have ethical concerns about the methods used to gather the information presented in the report. They may believe that the organization responsible for the report engaged in unethical practices or failed to consider important ethical considerations in their research, leading them to question the integrity of the report.

Additionally, they may have ideological differences with the conclusions drawn in the report. They may have a different perspective on the topic at hand or different beliefs about the best course of action to take, leading them to dissent from the report's recommendations.

Overall, a member of the organization responsible for this document may have principled, substantive reasons to dissent from this report based on concerns about bias, accuracy, ethics, or ideology.

Red Team Critique

This document appears to be a list of references related to psychological operations between the United States and the Soviet Union. However, it lacks any substantive analysis or discussion of the content of these references.

First, the document lacks context or explanation for why these references were chosen or how they relate to each other. It simply lists various sources without providing any indication of their significance or relevance to the topic of psychological operations between the US and the Soviet Union.

Second, the document is lacking in detail and depth. It simply lists the title of the references without providing any summary or analysis of their content. This makes it difficult for the reader to understand the key points or arguments made in these sources.

Additionally, the document is outdated, as it was published in It is important to consider more current sources when conducting research on a topic as sensitive and evolving as psychological operations between major world powers.

Overall, this document is not useful as a standalone resource for understanding psychological operations between the United States and the Soviet Union. It would benefit from more detailed analysis, context, and a focus on more current sources.

MAGA Perspective

This document is just more liberal propaganda trying to demonize the United States and prop up the Soviet Union. It's no surprise that it was published during the Carter administration, a time when America was weakened and vulnerable to communist influence. The idea that the United States would engage in psychological operations against the Soviet Union is absurd - we were always the victims of their deceit and manipulation.

The fact that this document was approved by the United States Congress just goes to show how deep the swamp really is. These politicians are more concerned with appeasing foreign enemies than standing up for American values. It's no wonder our country was in decline during this time, with weak leadership like this at the helm.

The United States Information Agency is just another example of the deep state working against the interests of true patriotic Americans. They were likely behind the dissemination of this document, spreading lies and misinformation to undermine our country and boost the Soviet Union. It's time to drain the swamp and get rid of these traitors who seek to weaken America from within.

The fact that this document even exists is a disgrace. It shows just how far our country had fallen by the 1970s, with communist sympathizers infiltrating our government and spreading their anti-American propaganda. We need to make America great again by purging these traitors and restoring our country to its former glory.

The United States Congress should be ashamed for allowing such a document to be published and disseminated. They are supposed to represent the American people, not push forward a liberal agenda that undermines our country's values and strength. It's time for real patriots to stand up and fight back against this kind of propaganda before it's too late.

Page-by-Page Summaries

BODY-1 *An overview of Psychological Operations (PSYOP) prepared by the Library of Congress in October 1989.*

BODY-2 *The page provides an overview of psychological operations (PSYOP) with a focus on military applications, including historical background, case studies, and current capabilities of the United States and Soviet Union.*

BODY-3 *The Federal Research Division of the Library of Congress offers fee-for-service research products to US government agencies, including studies, reports, and bibliographies on a wide range of subjects. Contact information provided for inquiries.*

BODY-4 *The page provides an overview of psychological operations (PSYOP) in history, focusing on Soviet and United States PSYOP tactics.*

BODY-5 *Overview of PSYOP, including definitions, historical applications, Soviet and US approaches, and the need for improvement in current policy.*

BODY-6 *PSYOP is a form of political and military activity aimed at influencing emotions, attitudes, beliefs, and behavior to achieve U.S. political and military objectives, as defined by DoD Directive S-3321.1. It includes planned psychological activities in peace and war to gain support and reduce hostility.*

BODY-7 *Psychological operations involve non-coercive methods to influence attitudes and actions of a targeted group, emphasizing credibility and truth as key elements for success. It acts as a force multiplier when used in combination with other military or political operations.*

BODY-8 *PSYOP evolved from psychological warfare to influence attitudes and actions of foreign groups in support of national objectives. It has been used strategically in international politics, particularly by ideologies like Communism and Fascism, leading to the development of disinformation and active measures.*

BODY-9 *The page discusses the expanded definition of propaganda, disinformation, and active measures in international PSYOP, highlighting the deceptive nature of disinformation and the broad scope of active measures in influencing foreign opinion and achieving political disruption on an international scale.*

BODY-10 *Propaganda is a tool used for managing attitudes through communication and symbols, with PSYOP propaganda requiring large amounts of true information. It is divided into white, gray, and black types, with symbolic propaganda using actions to convey messages. PSYOP relies on exploiting the target's capacity for self-deception.*

BODY-11 *Psychological operations target groups to shape perceptions and behavior, reducing the need for coercive action. PSYOPs differ from military deception, focusing on exploiting psychological vulnerabilities for long-term advantage.*

BODY-12 *The page discusses the use of psychological operations to influence group members, split nations from superpowers, and justify positions to domestic and foreign audiences. It highlights the importance of accurate evaluation of adversary psychology and the integration of PSYOP procedures with military preparedness.*

BODY-13 *PSYOP is crucial in superpower confrontations in weak areas with valuable resources, as seen in El Salvador, Cambodia, and Afghanistan. Successful counterinsurgency depends on understanding and exploiting the psychology of the local population. Ayatollah Khomeini's insurgency in Iran highlights the power of propaganda.*

BODY-14	*The importance of psychological operations in modern combat, integrating PSYOP into military doctrine, and using propaganda to rally domestic support for political and military causes.*
BODY-15	*Historical examples demonstrate diverse goals, methods, and target groups of psychological operations. Soviet and US PSYOP strategies are compared, highlighting the ideological battle between the two nations. Sun Tzu's Art of War illustrates the power of psychological tactics in warfare.*
BODY-16	*Historical examples of successful psychological warfare tactics, such as exaggerating army size and distributing propaganda leaflets, demonstrate the effectiveness of manipulating enemy psychology to gain military advantage.*
BODY-17	*World War I propaganda, particularly by the British, utilized print, radio, and film to spread rumors of German atrocities and undermine German morale, contributing to the Allied victory. The Creel Committee in the US was a model for wartime propaganda agencies.*
BODY-18	*Germans underestimated U.S. retaliation, leading to morale decline. Nazis used propaganda to manipulate public opinion, focusing on symbols and emotions. Hitler symbolized power and Goebbels convinced of enemies and Fascism. Peace desire hindered rational evaluation. Propaganda included rallies, media, and subversive groups.*
BODY-19	*Soviet PSYOP during the Cold War was based on Lenin's teachings, viewing the USSR in a constant war with the capitalist world. It was intense, complex, and backed by the political system to achieve Communist domination.*
BODY-20	*Soviet PSYOP campaigns use a mix of conventional and covert tactics to shape international dialogue in their favor, portraying the West as the aggressor and themselves as victims. They attribute all active measures to the US and its allies, aiming to control the narrative.*
BODY-21	*Soviet foreign policy influenced by unique International Department, propaganda split between agencies, KGB handles espionage and disinformation, increased focus on PSYOP activities during government reform.*
BODY-22	*Soviet active measures use forged documents and media stories to divide and manipulate target groups, with a focus on exploiting Western psychological vulnerabilities and promoting Soviet reforms. Cuba and the World Peace Council are key players in these operations.*
BODY-23	*Soviet active measures involve using personal contacts and propaganda to influence foreign decision-making institutions, exploiting weaknesses and promoting Soviet foreign policy goals. Examples include planting documents and creating propaganda to discredit opponents and advance Soviet interests.*
BODY-24	*Soviet Union's propaganda efforts in China backfired, leading to failed attempts to improve Sino-Soviet relations. The invasion of Afghanistan and shooting down of a Korean airliner further damaged Soviet credibility, with poorly coordinated propaganda failing to sway world opinion.*
BODY-25	*Gorbachev uses charismatic leadership and strategic messaging to reshape the Soviet Union's image, blending truth with propaganda to appeal to global audiences while continuing Lenin's political warfare tactics.*
BODY-26	*Soviet Union utilizes PSYOP extensively, blending propaganda with government functions, while United States faces challenges in countering Soviet influence through strategic messaging.*

BODY-27	*The page discusses the use of psychological operations (PSYOP) by the United States in various conflicts, highlighting challenges in coordination and effectiveness. It also mentions the role of charismatic leadership and the creation of PSYOP agencies during World War II.*
BODY-28	*PSYOP missions in World War II were hindered by disorganization, but the OWI's propaganda targeted enemy psychology effectively. Post-war, propaganda was associated with Fascism and Communism, leading to indecision about PSYOP in peacetime. The Korean War prompted the formation of centralized agencies for PSYOP.*
BODY-29	*Post-World War II, US focused on PSYOP due to Cold War threats. CIA created for covert activities. US faced challenges countering Soviet propaganda in Third World. Success mixed due to systemic differences.*
BODY-30	*Comparison of Soviet and American propaganda tactics, highlighting the challenges and successes of US psychological operations in the Vietnam War and the Dominican Republic.*
BODY-31	*PSYOP activities in Vietnam and Europe were successful, but budget cuts led to disbandment of Army units. Ft. Bragg became the main source of PSYOP support for military operations. Experts suggest expanding US capability and integrating PSYOP expertise into military training.*
BODY-32	*Increased emphasis on information as a national power element led to more overt psychological operations, including training and support for allied forces. Programs like the one in El Salvador have resulted in significant changes in approach to insurgency and human rights. Operations are coordinated with State Department and USIA.*
BODY-33	*The page discusses the role of covert and overt propaganda in US operations, focusing on public diplomacy efforts to improve international image and counter Soviet propaganda. Despite some improvements, coordination between policy agencies and public diplomacy remains a challenge.*
BODY-34	*US agencies disseminate propaganda worldwide, including the Voice of America and Radio Free Europe. In 1985, the Secretary of Defense created a Master Plan to revitalize PSYOP due to recognized deficiencies.*
BODY-35	*PSYOP underwent significant modernization and restructuring, including improved equipment, training, and staff organization, leading to a proactive approach and increased preparedness across various conflict scenarios. This progress necessitated a new plan by 1989 to accommodate the changes.*
BODY-36	*The United States has historically practiced psychological operations during times of military or diplomatic necessity, but has been reluctant to maintain PSYOP units during peacetime. There is a lack of overall coordination and training in PSYOP within the military, despite increasing need in counterinsurgency situations.*
BODY-37	*PSYOP principles remain valuable in military operations, encompassing various methods and activities. Credibility, positive messaging, and integration into broader programs are key. Widely practiced, with varying perceptions and effectiveness across nations, highlighting the importance of consistency and coordination.*
BODY-38	*PSYOP tactics are crucial for influencing neutral nations, especially in a world where conventional military operations are costly, nuclear war looms, and psychological warfare is cost-effective and prevalent. Military commanders must understand the psychology of conflict.*

BODY-39 *Various sources on military psychological operations, propaganda, and deception are cited, providing insight into the history and strategies used in these areas.*

BODY-40 *Various sources discussing Soviet propaganda, psychological warfare, and active measures, including insights from the United States Congress, New York Times Magazine, and other publications.*

BODY-41 *Various authors discuss military psychological operations, organizational strategy, public diplomacy, and political warfare in relation to U.S. foreign policy and low-intensity conflicts.*

Notable Passages

BODY-6 *"To subdue the enemy without fighting is the acme of skill."— Sun Tzu, 4th century B.C.*

BODY-7 *"The most critical element is credibility—to retain the attention of the audience, the audience must be convinced it is receiving information that is reliable and pertinent to its interests. If the audience detects contradictions or falsehoods, credibility is lost~for a particular operation, and perhaps for future operations as well. Therefore, the cardinal motto for all PSYOP applications is 'Truth is the best PSYOP.'"*

BODY-8 *Psychological warfare is thus the type of psychological operation most closely connected with military actions: before and during engagement, to minimize the enemy will to fight, and afterwards, to underscore the impact of his losses and the hopelessness of his situation. Military actions themselves (the dropping of the atomic bomb, as an extreme example) may play a psychological role beyond their military impact, because the demonstrated ability to inflict harm has a psychological effect on the potential victim.*

BODY-9 *"Disinformation, translated from the Russian term dezinformatsiya, has been defined as 'any government-sponsored communication in which deliberately misleading information is passed to targeted individuals, groups, or governments with the purpose of influencing foreign elite or public opinion.' Disinformation differs from propaganda because the latter does not necessarily involve deceiving a target group, and because disinformation always has a specific foreign target."*

BODY-10 *"Symbolic propaganda" uses action rather than words to produce its effect. The most dramatic example of symbolic propaganda was the use of the atomic bomb in World War II to physically demonstrate the hopelessness of the Japanese position. Several years later, the first Soviet nuclear test sent a symbolic message that had a strong psychological effect on the West.*

BODY-11 *Every identifiable group, society, and nation has a unique set of needs and goals, as well as a uniquely shaped group psychology. The needs and goals may be long- or short-term, military or political, real or imaginary. To cite two extreme examples, the group psychology may be shared by a small group in a short-term, tactical situation (such as a military unit occupying foreign territory), or by several nations in a semi-permanent, strategic situation (such as a group of nations strategically located between two superpowers). Between those extremes are many combinations of needs and goals. If a psychological operation is done properly, the perceptions formed by the target group can be slanted in a particular direction without immediate challenge and actions or attitudes changed accordingly.*

BODY-12 *"If such a message penetrates without effective challenge, it blunts the effectiveness of the occupation. This approach might be accompanied by terrorists acts that 'emphasize' the alienation of the occupiers."*

BODY-13 *"Victory goes to the side that best understands and exploits the psychology of the indigenous population that is the main source of support for the guerrillas."*

BODY-14 *"When the clear boundaries of open combat disappear and civilian populations become an integral part of every confrontation, PSYOP no longer is a specialized, sinister weapon that can be disregarded because it does not yield spectacular results. Proper PSYOP procedure is often a critical guarantee of success; solid PSYOP approaches to an indigenous population can hold territory with minimal expense or loss of life."*

BODY-15 *"An army of superior numbers can be 'made not to fight.' This idea was in use even before that time. An early example is the slaying of Holophernes, leader of an Assyrian force invading ancient Israel, by the Israelite Judith. Knowing that enemy troop morale depended heavily on the single figure of the commander, Judith gained the confidence of Holophernes, beheaded him, and carried the head back to her people. The symbolism of the missing head and the lost command figure totally demoralized the Assyrians, who were easily routed in spite of vastly superior numbers."*

BODY-16 *"Because the Mongols created an image of total, barbaric domination, target groups never believed they were the victims of astute psychological warfare. Once the image had spread, the Mongols had created a permanent weakness in enemy psychology, and thus gained a military advantage wherever the Mongol reputation was known."*

BODY-17 *Because of the expanded scale on which it was used, PSYOP is considered by historians as a crucial factor in the Allied victory in World War I. The Creel Committee, the first specialized U.S. agency for wartime propaganda, succeeded in building domestic support for a war that was not popular initially; it also was the model for later U.S. publicity and propaganda agencies. And the very presence of the U.S. in the war, after long neutrality, had great psychological as well as the military impact.*

BODY-18 *The charismatic figure of Adolph Hitler provided the ultimate symbol of renewed power to a nation humiliated by the results of World War I. The propaganda machine of Joseph Goebbels convinced Germans and many audiences elsewhere that Communists and Jews were the enemies; that only Fascism could provide protection from them; and that the advance of Fascism was both just and inevitable.*

BODY-19 *"The central concept (which sharply differentiates Soviet from United States approaches to the subject) is that the Soviet Union is in a state of undeclared war with capitalist world--a war that will not end until world Communist domination is achieved. Given the magnitude of the goal, moral constraints have had much less influence on Soviet PSYOP than on those of the United States and other countries."*

BODY-20 *A favorite message in the Soviet arsenal says that it is the West that is on the psychological offensive: with an insatiable ideological drive, imperialism uses all possible psychological means to undermine the progressive development of other nations toward the ideal, inevitable Communist order.*

BODY-21 *The disinformation mission aims mainly at destabilizing and misleading the NATO alliance and Japan, while concealing actual Soviet policy aims.*

BODY-22 *Active measures aim to divide the target group (most often NATO) by intensifying latent hostilities within it. Germany is a favorite target for such divisive methods because the Nazi past remains a psychological weak point for all of Europe. Print and broadcast media are nearly always used to achieve maximum dissemination of a message. The procedure is to identify a potentially sympathetic audience with political influence (for example, the leftist West German Green Party and the Labor Party in Great Britain), and tailor the message for maximum favor with that audience.*

BODY-23 *"Because the Soviet Union is the initiator, it has been able to choose its 'battlefields,' where chances of achieving psychological influence are greatest and opponents can be put on the defensive. In target countries, such campaigns exploit weak points such as ethnic rivalries, distrust of existing social or government systems, and class antagonism."*

BODY-24 *The obvious fabrications and confusion in the propaganda line violated the basic principle that information used in PSYOP must be believable to the target group. Historically, Soviet active measures have had several weaknesses. The Soviet ideology of atheism and Communism is unattractive to many audiences, so it must be concealed or glossed over in many cases. Acts such as the Afghan invasion have eroded trust in the Soviet Union as defender of Third-World liberty. And many forgeries and press placements have been poorly executed and very obvious.*

BODY-25 *Gorbachev is able to send direct, credible messages to world leaders and use international media to propagate a view of the Soviet Union as a reformed, peace-loving, and benign nation. Like Roosevelt, he has cultivated a personal image of honest and moral humanity that has universal appeal. Arms control proposals, slipshod and obviously insincere under previous regimes, now impress even Western skeptics with their scope and consistency. Gorbachev has also shown wisdom in choosing and shaping his messages to target audiences, alternating between firmness and conciliation.*

BODY-26 *In summary, the Soviet Union is by far the largest practitioner of PSYOP in the world. PSYOP has been an integral part of its foreign and domestic policy since the Bolshevik Revolution. In organizational structure and function, Soviet psychological operations overlap the more conventional functions of government and diplomatic institutions. Because PSYOP is still viewed as another version of military struggle, coordination of tactical military doctrine with long-term strategic-international goals remains especially close and consistent.*

BODY-27 *"Since mass communications became a PSYOP tool, the United States has been involved in several wars requiring domestic and international justification of its position versus adversaries such as the Germans, the Japanese, the Koreans and Chinese, and the Viet Cong. In each conflict, large-scale tactical PSYOP machinery also went into motion."*

BODY-28 *"The propaganda of the OWI was marked by careful evaluation of target psychology, appropriate messages, and effective delivery. For example, the OWI aimed surrender appeals at the psychological vulnerabilities of fanatical Japanese soldiers, inducing large numbers to surrender in spite of a military code that seemingly precluded such behavior."*

BODY-29 *In general, withdrawal from PSYOP activity after World War II was slowed by the realization that the Soviet Union was now a formidable enemy in the Cold War. This realization was based on two ideas: that the world does not automatically understand or approve of the United States; and that the Soviet Union is ready and able to exploit doubts about the morality and motives of the United States, in numerous overt and covert ways.*

BODY-30 *The Vietnam War was the most recent large-scale PSYOP campaign of the United States. As in Korea, the main tactical devices were loudspeakers, leaflets, and radio. The Chien-Hoi (Open Arms) amnesty program stressed the strength of the South Vietnamese Army and the hopelessness of the Viet Cong position. In many respects, this massive effort fell short on both strategic and tactical levels: the first when domestic and international doubts about legitimacy were not met by United States official information, the second when PSYOP and military operations failed to complement each other, and the enemy was able to exploit the psychological vulnerabilities of both United States troops and the indigenous population of Vietnam.*

BODY-31 *CounterPSYOPs activity in Europe in the early 1980s ensured timely installation of intermediate-range missiles, despite an intensive Soviet psychological campaign to exploit European peace and antinuclear groups.*

BODY-32 *Since the Reagan Administration put additional emphasis on information as one of the elements of national power, overt psychological operations in peacetime have been increased. These psychological operations have included training and advice to indigenous forces allied with the United States, surveys and assessments leading to actual operations, miscellaneous support to host nation PSYOP programs, and other overt PSYOP projects. Typical of PSYOP support to host nation programs is the long-term program created for El Salvador. One trainer is assigned to the U.S. military group in the capital, San Salvador, to coordinate all U.S. PSYOP programs in the country.*

BODY-33 *"In the 1980s, the United States has sought to bolster programs of cultural relations and positive image-making abroad. 'Public diplomacy' has been used much more aggressively to correct the record about United States intentions and in counterattacking Soviet and Cuban propaganda."*

BODY-34 *"There is an 'American suspicion of the tools of psychological manipulation,' which insulates American institutions from association with such activities."*

BODY-35 *"Heightened preparedness for wartime, contingency situations, low-intensity conflict, and peacetime operations resulted from the changes initiated from the Master Plan. By 1989, the response to the Master Plan had so changed the PSYOP environment that a new plan was needed to accommodate the progress made since 1985."*

BODY-36 *"Although efforts were made periodically toward a comprehensive U.S. tactical PSYOP doctrine, the policy has been to approach each case individually after it arises, with no overall philosophical context."*

BODY-37 *The time-honored principles of PSYOP retain exactly the same basic value as they have always had: as a force multiplier that complements military operations by lessening the determination of the target to resist. But since the days of Genghis Khan the definition of PSYOP has come to include a much broader range of activities and methods: from organized campaigns using leaflets and speakers in conventional tactical combat, to official statements by national leaders aimed at an international audience, to the everyday interaction of non-specialized military personnel with a host population.*

BODY-38 *Under these conditions the psychology of conflict assumes a primary role, one that must be understood by every military commander.*

BODY-41 *Joseph Miranda. "Political Warfare: Can the West Survive?" Journal of Social, Political and Economic Studies, Spring 1985, p. 7.*

AN OVERVIEW OF
PSYCHOLOGICAL OPERATIONS (PSYOP)

Prepared by:
Federal Research Division
Library of Congress
Washington, DC 20540
October 1989
Analyst: Glenn Curtis

REPORT DOCUMENTATION PAGE

Form Approved
OMB No. 0704-0188

1. AGENCY USE ONLY (*Leave Blank*)	2. REPORT DATE	3. REPORT TYPE AND DATES COVERED
	October 1989	Final

4. TITLE AND SUBTITLE

An Overview of Psychological Operations (PSYOP)

5. FUNDING NUMBERS

6. AUTHOR(S)

Glenn Curtis

7. PERFORMING ORGANIZATION NAME(S) AND ADDRESS(ES)

Federal Research Division
Library of Congress
Washington, DC 20540-5220

8. PERFORMING ORGANIZATION REPORT NUMBER

9. SPONSORING/MONITORING AGENCY NAME(S) AND ADDRESS(ES)

N/A

10. SPONSORING/MONITORING AGENCY REPORT NUMBER

11. SUPPLEMENTARY NOTES

Prepared under an Interagency Agreement

12a. DISTRIBUTION/AVAILABILITY STATEMENT

Approved for public release; distribution unlimited.

12b. DISTRIBUTION CODE

13. ABSTRACT (*Maximum 200 words*)

This study examines the theory and application of psychological operations (PSYOP), with particular emphasis on contemporary military applications. Substantial historical and theoretical background is supplied, with detailed analysis of case studies. Current PSYOP applications by the United States and the Soviet Union are emphasized and include descriptions of their respective PSYOP capabilities, organizations, and goals.

14. SUBJECT TERMS

Psychological operations
United States
Soviet Union

15. NUMBER OF PAGES

36

16. PRICE CODE

17. SECURITY CLASSIFICATION OF REPORT	18. SECURITY CLASSIFICATION OF THIS PAGE	19. SECURITY CLASSIFICATION OF ABSTRACT	20. LIMITATION OF ABSTRACT
UNCLASSIFIED	UNCLASSIFIED	UNCLASSIFIED	SAR

NSN 7540-01-280-5500

Standard Form 298 (Rev. 2-89)
Prescribed by ANSI Std 239-18
298-102

Dear Reader:

This product was prepared by the staff of the *Federal Research Division* of the *Library of Congress* under an interagency agreement with the sponsoring United States Government agency.

The Federal Research Division is the Library of Congress's primary fee-for-service research unit. At the request of Executive and Judicial branch agencies of the United States Government and on a cost-recovery basis, the Division prepares studies and reports, chronologies, bibliographies, foreign-language abstracts, and other tailored products in hard-copy and electronic media. The subjects researched include the broad spectrum of social sciences, physical sciences, and the humanities.

For additional information on obtaining the research and analytical services of the Federal Research Division, please call 202/707-9905, fax 202/707-9920), via Internet frd@mail.loc.gov, or write to *Marketing Coordinator, Federal Research Division, Library of Congress, Washington, DC 20540-5220.*

Louis R. Mortimer
Chief
Federal Research Division
Library of Congress
Washington, DC 20540-5220

CONTENTS

OUTLINE

1. INTRODUCTION AND DEFINITIONS

    A. Definitions of PSYOP, official and unofficial
    B. Expansion of scope in the twentieth century
    C. New concepts: disinformation, active measures
    D. Propaganda
    E. How the mechanisms of PSYOP work, with examples
    F. New applications--low-intensity conflict, unconventional warfare
    G. Domestic applications--rallying public support

2. PSYOP APPLICATIONS IN HISTORY

    A. Judith and Holophernes
    B. Ghengis Khan
    C. American Revolution propaganda
    D. World War I and the beginning of PSYOP expansion
    E. Nazi propaganda
    F. The postwar situation

3. SOVIET PSYOP

    A. Philosophical base
    B. General methodology of the Soviet PSYOP approach
    C. The Soviets PSYOP machinery
        1. International Department
        2. Propaganda Department
        3. KGB
    D. Active measures and how they work--examples
    E. Soviet propaganda failures
    F The program under Gorbachev
        1. New approaches
        2. Old approaches continued

4. UNITED STATES PSYOP

    A. The contemporary environment
    B. Historical background, beginning with World War II
    C. The U.S. PSYOP record
    D. Needs for improvement in current policy

5. CONCLUSIONS

6. ENDNOTES

1. INTRODUCTION AND DEFINITIONS

"To subdue the enemy without fighting is the acme of skill."--
Sun Tzu, 4th century B.C.

Psychological operations, or PSYOP, is a form of political and military activity that is understood and defined in a number of different ways. The definition upon which current peacetime U.S. PSYOP policy is based was established in Department of Defense Directive S-3321.1, Overt Psychological Operations Conducted by the Military Services in Peacetime and in Contingencies Short of Declared War (1984). That definition states that Psychological Operations are "planned political, economic, military, and ideological activities directed toward foreign countries, organizations, and individuals in order to create emotions, attitudes, understandings, beliefs, or behavior favorable to the achievement of U.S. political and military objectives." The DoD directive was formulated to establish standard guidelines for all aspects of PSYOP (planning, programming, execution, control) conducted by agencies of the U.S. Department of Defense in non-wartime conditions. But PSYOP also includes a number of other activities that fall under strategic military and political policy. Activities of that type are defined in Joint Chiefs of Staff Publication 1 as: "planned psychological activities in peace and war, which normally pursue objectives to gain the support and cooperation of friendly and neutral countries and to reduce the will and the capacity of hostile or potentially hostile countries to wage war." The latter definition reflects the expansion in scope that has occurred in PSYOP in the last fifty years. In the modern world, the scope of PSYOP is wider than ever before, even though the basic concepts continue as they have existed for thousands of years. Reflecting this expansion, PSYOP expert Fred W. Walker notes, "We might consider the term persuasive communications to mean the same thing as psychological operations."[1] Another expert, William Daugherty, prescribes an even broader field: "PSYOP is communication and therefore covers the entire field of human action."[2] In the present political-military meaning of the term, PSYOP is a multi-stage process that uses a combination of non-coercive devices to gain influence over the actions and attitudes of a targeted group without resorting to the use of force. The first stage of the process is defining the target, the second is finding methods or agents to influence the target's perception of reality, and the third is the output of the message through selected channels. In this process, the most critical element is credibility--to retain the attention of the audience, the audience must be convinced it is receiving information that is reliable and pertinent to its interests. If the audience detects contradictions or falsehoods, credibility is lost--for a particular operation, and perhaps for future operations as well. Therefore, the cardinal motto for all PSYOP applications is "Truth is the best PSYOP." The advantage of using PSYOP has remained the same throughout its history: if an opponent's attitude can be influenced favorably, his physical resistance will diminish. This means that, when used in combination with other military or political operations, PSYOP acts as a force multiplier, enhancing the effect of those operations on the target.

The term "psychological operations" was first used in reference to surrender messages (messages offering humane treatment for enemy personnel ceasing to resist U.S. forces) sent to the Japanese mainland in 1945. From World War I until the 1960s, "psychological warfare" was the umbrella term in common use. In the 1960s, it was recognized that much more was included in the modern concept than warfare in the conventional sense, so PSYOP became the umbrella term. Psychological warfare, or PSYWAR, remains part of the PSYOP concept. It refers to activity seeking to influence the attitudes and actions of hostile foreign groups in support of national objectives in wartime.[3] Psychological warfare is thus the type of psychological operation most closely connected with military actions: before and during engagement, to minimize the enemy will to fight, and afterwards, to underscore the impact of his losses and the hopelessness of his situation. Military actions themselves (the dropping of the atomic bomb, as an extreme example) may play a psychological role beyond their military impact, because the demonstrated ability to inflict harm has a psychological effect on the potential victim.

In the twentieth century, PSYOP applications have been broadened by the intense ideologies and systems of mass communications that have supported them since World War I. Particularly since the 1930s, the connection of PSYOP with ideology and mass communication has made it a constant strategic element of international politics. Communism and Fascism have used PSYOP in new ways, still considered unethical by much of the world, and forced the opponents of their ideologies to rethink their PSYOP procedures accordingly. The concepts of "disinformation" and "active measures" have been added to the international PSYOP vocabulary, and the definition of "propaganda" has been expanded in this process.

Disinformation, translated from the Russian term dezinformatsiya, has been defined as "any government-sponsored communication in which deliberately misleading information is passed to targeted individuals, groups, or governments with the purpose of influencing foreign elite or public opinion." Disinformation differs from propaganda because the latter does not necessarily involve deceiving a target group, and because disinformation always has a specific foreign target.[4] "Active measures" is a translation of an umbrella Soviet term, aktivnyye meropriyatiya. It has come into English usage because our term "covert activities" does not cover the enormous breadth of activities and participants included in the Soviet concept. In addition to using conventional covert operations, active measures seek to acquire influence over an opponent's attitudes through the media, economic leverage, front organizations, and other seemingly innocent overt agencies with covert sponsorship.[5] The goal of active measures can be summarized as political influence and disruption on an international scale, to achieve a specific result. Both disinformation and active measures are weapons in what Communist dogma sees as peacetime psychological warfare. That warfare is an extension of the international military goals of the Communist movement. Those weapons will be discussed more fully in the Soviet PSYOP section of this survey. But it is important to note that these types of PSYOP have been added only to the Soviet arsenal. While the U.S. must respond effectively to them, it remains committed to the principle of truth in all information programs.

"Propaganda" is a broad term that means management of collective attitudes through communications and symbols, for the purpose of promoting or damaging a cause.[6] Among its non-PSYOP applications are commercial advertising, political campaigning, and religious exhortation. (The term was invented by the Roman Catholic Church in its seventeenth-century campaigns against Protestantism.) But in the contemporary public understanding, those aspects have been over-shadowed by the widespread political uses of propaganda in the twentieth century. Although the term had become associated with untruth, propaganda in the PSYOP context must contain large amounts of true information, because of the primary requirement that the audience believe the message. By convention, PSYOP propaganda is divided into three types: white, gray, and black. White propaganda originates from a correctly identified source, black from a completely misidentified source; the source of gray propaganda is masked by transmission through a "front" agency that is nominally independent of the actual source. "Symbolic propaganda" uses action rather than words to produce its effect. The most dramatic example of symbolic propaganda was the use of the atomic bomb in World War II to physically demonstrate the hopelessness of the Japanese position. Several years later, the first Soviet nuclear test sent a symbolic message that had a strong psychological effect on the West.

PSYOP relies heavily on correct evaluation and exploitation of the target's "capacity for self-deception."[7] What is this "capacity for self-deception," and how is it exploited? Approaches differ according to specific conditions, because target groups vary widely. Examples of such target groups are military enemies, political rivals, indigenous populations in guerrilla and counterinsurgency operations, and domestic populations whose support is needed for military or political campaigns. Every identifiable group, society, and nation has a unique set of needs and goals, as well as a uniquely shaped group psychology. The needs and goals may be long- or short-term, military or political, real or imaginary. To cite two extreme examples, the group psychology may be shared by a small group in a short-term, tactical situation (such as a military unit occupying foreign territory), or by several nations in a semi-permanent, strategic situation (such as a group of nations strategically located between two superpowers). Between those extremes are many combinations of needs and goals. If a psychological operation is done properly, the perceptions formed by the target group can be slanted in a particular direction without immediate challenge and actions or attitudes changed accordingly. Psychological operations thus can reduce the risk and expense of coercive action. Such operations are especially useful to groups such as guerrilla forces whose capacity for coercive action is limited. PSYOPs is not to be confused with military deception, which causes an enemy to take inappropriate action by misleading his assessment of positions or intentions.

For the operating side, the immediate target is a weak point of an ultimate target, a place where psychological advantage can be gained and used as a weapon in the longer term. How would this work in the two examples given above? For an occupying force, the points of psychological vulnerability might be distance from home and prolonged exposure to an uncomfortable cultural environment. In such a case, if the opponent's intelligence reveals discontent within the force, a psychological operation might use communications media to convince group members of the loneliness and pointlessness of their venture, and to offer easy surrender conditions. If such a message penetrates without effective challenge, it blunts the effectiveness of the occupation. This approach might be accompanied by terrorists acts that "emphasize" the alienation of the occupiers.

In the international example, smaller nations are subjected to constant superpower propaganda. The Soviet Union uses overt and covert measures in campaigns to split smaller countries from the United States and move them toward a neutral position. In Europe such efforts exploit the substantial public and official desire for peace and security, doubts about American resolve to defend Europe, and fears of nuclear war. A campaign of this sort continues over many years and is woven into the fabric of superpower foreign policy.

In modern times nations increasingly understand the need for propaganda to justify their positions to both domestic and foreign audiences. In peacetime and in protracted war, PSYOP procedures now are integrated with and parallel to measures of military preparedness. Key factors in their success are accurate evaluation of adversary psychology, secrecy, and the output of information that is consistent and credible.

A PSYOP application of particular current value is in insurgency and counterinsurgency activity in what is called "low-intensity conflict" (LIC). Geographically confined to the Third World, LIC PSYOP now is often used in confrontations of client groups of larger powers such as

Soviet Union, China, and the United States. Such confrontations occur most often in areas with weak governments, poorly developed or unbalanced economies, and valuable natural resources or strategic location.[8] In recent years, El Salvador, Cambodia, and Afghanistan have been the sites of major superpower insurgency-counterinsurgency efforts. The U.S. has been on both sides of such campaigns, aiding counterinsurgency in El Salvador and the Philippines, insurgency in Nicaragua and Angola. Because guerrilla warfare relies heavily on psychological impact to complement sheer force, successful counterinsurgency must use PSYOP effectively to defeat such campaigns. Victory goes to the side that best understands and exploits the psychology of the indigenous population that is the main source of support for the guerrillas. As insurgency and counterinsurgency have developed, important PSYOP tools are community relations programs, public information, and civic action programs carried out by military personnel in the areas in dispute. Insurgency PSYOP is not limited to proxy confrontations between the United States and Soviet camps. The Ayatollah Khomeini conducted a very effective insurgency against the Iranian government. Exploiting religious fervor and dissatisfaction with the government, the exiled Khomeini smuggled large numbers of tape cassettes into Iran, spreading propaganda to stir revolutionary feeling and build a movement from an initially small number of followers.[9] In this case, no effective counterinsurgency campaign was mounted, and the government fell.

In the contemporary world, unconventional warfare is the rule, not the exception. Given that fact, PSYOP has become a military tool of greater importance than it was in the "classic" model. This is because the element of psychology is present in all forms and levels of combat, even when some conventional aspects of doctrine become less relevant. When the clear boundaries of open combat disappear and civilian populations become an integral part of every confrontation, PSYOP no longer is a specialized, sinister weapon that can be disregarded because it does not yield spectacular results. Proper PSYOP procedure is often a critical guarantee of success; solid PSYOP approaches to an indigenous population can hold territory with minimal expense or loss of life. But under such circumstances, the PSYOP weapons must be as familiar as any other weapon to all military personnel, because it is they who carry out PSYOP in their everyday contact with the population. In places such as El Salvador, the psychological relationship between military personnel and the civilian population is a prime determinant of the government's success against guerrillas; in this case, U.S. advisers are training the host nation's forces in PSYOP applications. A key word is "integration" of PSYOP into the framework of conventional military doctrine.

Another important application of PSYOP is to rally a domestic population behind a political or military cause. In wartime all nations, whatever their political system, must inspire willing sacrifice by their people. All U.S. war efforts, from the American Revolution to Vietnam, have required extensive "selling." As Korea and Vietnam showed, the complex psychology of a democracy is not always receptive to such campaigns. In such cases, targeted propaganda is the most important tool, but covert active measures have also been useful for totalitarian governments in combating uncooperative internal elements.

The historical examples that follow will show the variety of goals, methods, agents, and target groups that have been included in psychological operations of the past. In the sections that follow, discussion of past and current Soviet PSYOP will show how that nation has refined and expanded the entire field to meet the ideological requirements of the Leninist state. And discussion of United States PSYOP, past and present, will focus on the response to Soviet PSYOP campaigns from World War II to the present, in what has become the most massive PSYOP battle in history.

2. PSYOP APPLICATIONS IN HISTORY

The Art of War, a treatise written by the Chinese military thinker Sun Tzu in the fourth century B.C., advocates the idea that an army of superior numbers can be "made not to fight." This idea was in use even before that time. An early example is the slaying of Holophernes, leader of an Assyrian force invading ancient Israel, by the Israelite Judith. Knowing that enemy troop morale depended heavily on the single figure of the commander, Judith gained the confidence of Holophernes, beheaded him, and carried the head back to her people. The symbolism of the missing head and the lost command figure totally demoralized the Assyrians, who were easily routed in spite of vastly superior numbers. The story appears in the apocryphal Biblical Book of Judith; its historical accuracy is unproven, but it remains a good example of assessing the enemy's psychological weak point and using a powerful psychological symbol to bolster the morale of one's own forces.[10]

In another example, Ghengis Khan is credited with leading huge hordes of savage horsemen across Russia and into Europe. The size of his armies was exaggerated by agents planted in advance of the army and by rumor and other forms of propaganda. To supplement his PSYOP activities, Ghengis Khan also used rapid troop maneuver to confirm the illusion of invincible numbers. Because the Mongols created an image of total, barbaric domination, target groups never believed they were the victims of astute psychological warfare. Once the image had spread, the Mongols had created a permanent weakness in enemy psychology, and thus gained a military advantage wherever the Mongol reputation was known.[11]

In another instance, during the American Revolution the rebels distributed propaganda leaflets that invited Hessian mercenaries and British common soldiers to desert. One such leaflet provided two short, contrasting lists: the negatives of life in the British Army and the advantages of deserting and settling permanently in America. Promises of leniency and surrender passes have become a staple of battlefield PSYOP. In the Revolutionary War application, the direct appeal exploited the mentality of the occupying force, class differences between officers and enlisted men, and nationality differences between the British and their German mercenaries. Thousands of troops heeded the appeal and never returned to Europe. At the same time, domestic loyalist opposition was muffled by anti-British propaganda in the newspapers of the thirteen colonies.[12]

A qualitative change occurred in PSYOP about l900, when communications became much faster and more inclusive. For the first time, entire nations could be targeted in a psychological operation by print, radio, and film. These media provided direct, reliable transmission of propaganda messages to anyone within sight or earshot. The new media were first used widely in World War I; the British used them to spread rumors of German atrocities, including cannibalism.[13] Because the British had already developed a more sophisticated print and communications system than the Germans, they mounted a propaganda campaign that the Germans could not overcome. The British diplomatic service was also more adept at public diplomacy than its German equivalent. The British used German propaganda ineptitude to their advantage by simply disseminating many undiplomatic German statements, without change or comment; the difference in PSYOP skill between the two sides was enough to make the message clear that the Germans were uncivilized, arrogant "Huns" (a term used by the Kaiser himself for his army). German morale was deflated by having bombastic public statements made into ammunition for the enemy. This propaganda defeat was an important incentive for better performance by German propagandists in the next war.

Because of the expanded scale on which it was used, PSYOP is considered by historians as a crucial factor in the Allied victory in World War I. The Creel Committee, the first specialized U.S. agency for wartime propaganda, succeeded in building domestic support for a war that was not popular initially; it also was the model for later U.S. publicity and propaganda agencies. And the very presence of the U.S. in the war, after long neutrality, had great psychological as well as the military impact. Early in 1917, Germany began sinking all ships approaching Britain, in order to starve the British into surrender. The

Germans assumed that Britain would surrender before the U.S. could retaliate for its sunken ships by entering the war on Britain's side; when the error of this gamble became obvious, German morale fell. The German General Ludendorff named allied PSYOP the most important factor in German morale decline.

Before and during World War II, the Nazis used a propaganda machine aimed first at domestic opinion, then at world opinion. The basic psychological assumption of that machine was that public opinion is formed by symbols and images, not rational thought. If the correct symbols were presented with enough force, the public would follow. The theory worked because the audiences chosen were prone to self-deception about certain emotional topics. The charismatic figure of Adolph Hitler provided the ultimate symbol of renewed power to a nation humiliated by the results of World War I. The propaganda machine of Joseph Goebbels convinced Germans and many audiences elsewhere that Communists and Jews were the enemies; that only Fascism could provide protection from them; and that the advance of Fascism was both just and inevitable.[14] The worldwide desire for peace provided a psychological weak point that prevented rational evaluation of these messages; British and United States opposition was delayed until Europe had been conquered piecemeal. By that stage, Germany had developed effective print and broadcast media. A much older form of propaganda dissemination, the mass rally, was also used very profitably. The Germans also made extensive use of "black propaganda" and subversive pro-Nazi groups and agents in occupied territory.

After World War II, the Soviet Union raised peacetime PSYOP to new levels of sophistication as the Cold War broke out. And, as new international political conditions developed, tactical military PSYOP began to play a new role. These activities will be the subject of the following sections.

3. SOVIET PSYOP

Like other aspects of Soviet policy, the Soviet theory of psychological operations is based on the teachings of Lenin. The central concept (which sharply differentiates Soviet from United States approaches to the subject) is that the Soviet Union is in a state of undeclared war with capitalist world--a war that will not end until world Communist domination is achieved. Given the magnitude of the goal, moral constraints have had much less influence on Soviet PSYOP than on those of the United States and other countries. In the words of covert operations specialist Chapman Pincher, for the Soviet Union "politics is the continuation of war by other means."[15] On the peacetime strategic level, politics is the main arena of Soviet PSYOP. However, this approach was not invented by the Bolsheviks in l9l7; it was used sporadically for centuries by the Russian tsars in domestic and foreign relations, but it has been codified and intensified in the last seven decades. Soviet PSYOP is by far the most intensive, complex and consistent peacetime campaign of its type ever launched. The Soviet political system backs its PSYOP policy with whatever resources are necessary to achieve its goals.

Soviet PSYOP campaigns are a tightly integrated combination of conventional devices, influential "legitimate" institutions such as the diplomatic corps and the press, and covert activities. On the level of open propaganda, the goal is to "out-talk" the adversary, establishing terms of international dialogue favorable to the Soviet Union. This process is constant, aimed at wearing down the West and convincing other listeners that the Soviet position is valid. A favorite message in the Soviet arsenal says that it is the West that is on the psychological offensive: with an insatiable ideological drive, imperialism uses all possible psychological means to undermine the progressive development of other nations toward the ideal, inevitable Communist order. Furthermore, Dmitri Volkogonov, the leading Soviet PSYOP theoretician, says that the imperialist powers invented psychological warfare to maintain world domination.[16] Briefly stated, his view is that imperialist PSYOP seeks to divide the communist world, disorient its people politically, and falsely portray the Soviet Union as the main threat to world peace. Volkogonov attributes virtually all the known Soviet active measures methodology to the United States and its imperialist allies. To the extent that this idea is believed around the world, Soviet PSYOP succeeds in putting the debate into its terms.

Three departments of the Soviet government supervise active measures and propaganda activities. The International Department of the Communist Party of the Soviet Union provides liaison with nonruling Communist parties and front organizations abroad, directs their active measures, and apportions responsibility for various types of activity. This department also suggests new measures to advance the international policies of the ruling Politburo. Overall foreign policy is often affected by activities of the International Department (I.D.), which has no equivalent in Western governments.[17] The functions of this agency appear to have been expanded and refined in recent years, especially after the abolishment of the party's International Information Department. A key figure in this development was Anatoli Dobrynin, former Ambassador to the U.S. and head of the I.D. until late 1988. The latter was in charge of the overall propaganda apparatus until l986, when that function was split between the I.D. and a second major agency, the Propaganda Department. The latter now runs all domestic and foreign propaganda efforts. Its level of sophistication rose especially fast under Aleksandr Yakovlev, who until reassigned late in l988 was an effective domestic and international spokesman for the Gorbachev reforms.[18] The third propaganda agency is the KGB, or Committee for State Security, which handles espionage and disinformation activities at home and abroad. The disinformation mission aims mainly at destabilizing and misleading the NATO alliance and Japan, while concealing actual Soviet policy aims. In addition to the three major agencies, the Ministry of Foreign Affairs has broad responsibility for the overt Soviet press and foreign cultural relations--which in the Soviet system are closely coordinated with less "legitimate" PSYOP functions.

Although government reform has changed some of the structure of this system, there is evidence that even more resources are now allocated to PSYOP activities. History has shown that active measures are emphasized in times of improved relations with the West because targets become more vulnerable in such times.[19]

Favorite covert devices of Soviet active measures are forged documents and planted media stories, surfacing in forms that erode the position of the ultimate target. Often, forged United States and NATO documents are used to show that the West is intent on aggression in Europe or the Third World. Active measures aim to divide the target group (most often NATO) by intensifying latent hostilities within it. Germany is a favorite target for such divisive methods because the Nazi past remains a psychological weak point for all of Europe. Print and broadcast media are nearly always used to achieve maximum dissemination of a message. The procedure is to identify a potentially sympathetic audience with political influence (for example, the leftist West German Green Party and the Labor Party in Great Britain), and tailor the message for maximum favor with that audience.[20] In recent years, this tailoring includes maximum exposure of the terms perestroika (restructuring) and glasnost (openness), which for the Western audience indicate that hoped-for Soviet internal reforms are taking place and Cold War tension is easing. Debate flourishes on the actuality of those reforms, but there is no doubt that the terminology used to describe them has been quite successful in exploiting a Western psychological preoccupation.

A variety of agencies--from individual covert agents to client nations--carry out Soviet psychological operations. In the Third World, Cuba is an especially active agent, working on Soviet operations and independently. A major front organization for Soviet operations is the Helsinki-based World Peace Council. That organization, indirectly controlled by the Communist Party of the Soviet Union, plays a major role in stirring anti-NATO feeling in Europe. Political influence operations are a special type of active measure, using personal contacts to advance a Soviet position in foreign decisionmaking institutions. These contacts range from foreign figures (diplomats, journalists, scientists) to KGB agents "planted" in positions of influence.[21] Because the Soviet Union is the initiator, it has been able to choose its "battlefields," where chances of achieving psychological influence are greatest and opponents can be put on the defensive. In target countries, such campaigns exploit weak points such as ethnic rivalries, distrust of existing social or government systems, and class antagonism. And active measures are always used in conjunction with other devices to advance Soviet foreign policy goals.

A few examples of Soviet active measures will demonstrate their goals and methods. In l976, a testament of Zhou En-lai surfaced in a prominent Japanese newspaper. The document spoke against the Cultural Revolution in China and advocated closer relations with the Soviet Union. It had been placed by the KGB office in Tokyo.[22] In another instance, the KGB created a pamphlet, entitled CIA Insider, purported to be a listing of CIA agents and press outlets all over the world. The pamphlet, released in Switzerland, attempted to show the pervasive CIA influence in the Western press; it is an example of the "upside-down" black propaganda ploy of attributing Soviet PSYOP methods to Western nations.[23] And in the early l960s, a long series of items planted in the European press ruined the political career of Franz-Josef Strauss, a staunch advocate of United States armaments in West Germany. Strauss was painted as a warmonger seeking revenge on the Soviet Union for the results of World War II.[24] In another example, in 1979, Radio Ba Yi began broadcasting into China from the Soviet Far East. Its positions on domestic, diplomatic and military issues aimed initially at discrediting Deng Xiaoping, who was also attacked directly by the station. The Soviet Union acknowledged no role in the broadcasts, which supported all Soviet positions and advocate closer Sino-Soviet relations.[25] In the recent Soviet effort for better relations with China, the station was shut down.

The Soviet Union has also found itself on the negative side of PSYOP activities. When it invaded Afghanistan, counterinsurgency efforts failed to win over the indigenous population, and the occupying force became demoralized by guerrilla psychological warfare. And in l983 the Soviet Union shot down a Korean civilian airliner, causing an uproar in world opinion. The Soviets tried to turn press attention "upside-down" by claiming that the United States had provoked the incident--but Soviet statements were poorly coordinated and contradictory, and they failed to win the battle of world opinion.[26] The obvious fabrications and confusion in the propaganda line violated the basic principle that information used in PSYOP must be believable to the target group.

Historically, Soviet active measures have had several weaknesses. The Soviet ideology of atheism and Communism is unattractive to many audiences, so it must be concealed or glossed over in many cases. Acts such as the Afghan invasion have eroded trust in the Soviet Union as defender of Third-World liberty. And many forgeries and press placements have been poorly executed and very obvious.[27]

Most experts on the Soviet Union agree that in recent years the sophistication of Soviet propaganda and active measures has grown, and some of their weaknesses have been eliminated. First, the Soviet Union now has a charismatic leader in the person of Mikhail Gorbachev. This is a weapon the Soviets have never had before. Gorbachev is able to send direct, credible messages to world leaders and use international media to propagate a view of the Soviet Union as a reformed, peace-loving, and benign nation. Like Roosevelt, he has cultivated a personal image of honest and moral humanity that has universal appeal. Following the cardinal principle of PSYOP, that all messages be based in truth, Gorbachev's messages utilize the actual liberalization of internal and external Soviet policy (highlighting such events as removal of Soviet tanks from Hungary and the liberation of Andrei Sakharov) to maximum effect in shaping the new image. Arms control proposals, slipshod and obviously insincere under previous regimes, now impress even Western skeptics with their scope and consistency. Gorbachev has also shown wisdom in choosing and shaping his messages to target audiences, alternating between firmness and conciliation. At the same time, there is strong evidence of continued commitment to Lenin's principle of all-out political war as an extension of military struggle in peacetime. A 1988 report of the United States Information Agency lists major active-measures "black" programs begun after Gorbachev came to power. Among the messages widely disseminated by these programs: the AIDS virus was created in an American laboratory for germ warfare; the United States developed a weapon that kills only non-whites; Latin American babies are butchered and sold to U.S. distributors for use in medical transplants; and the CIA murdered Swedish Prime Minister Olaf Palme. While such messages have not changed substantially since earlier years, the approach of more subtle, "gray" programs has changed. Soviet-controlled international peace groups now seek a broader appeal by softening their rhetoric; other Soviet-influenced groups now seek wide contact with Westerners, to subtly convince them that Soviet positions are just; and the Soviets now sponsor many international peace forums, including respected professional figures, to enhance their peace-loving image. All these efforts complement the statements and actions of Gorbachev, whose programs of glasnost and perestroika seem committed to greater Soviet openness and nonmilitary programs.[28]

In summary, the Soviet Union is by far the largest practitioner of PSYOP in the world. PSYOP has been an integral part of its foreign and domestic policy since the Bolshevik Revolution. In organizational structure and function, Soviet psychological operations overlap the more conventional functions of government and diplomatic institutions. Because PSYOP is still viewed as another version of military struggle, coordination of tactical military doctrine with long-term strategic-international goals remains especially close and consistent.

4. UNITED STATES PSYOP

In the "age of communications," all nations must find ways to "explain themselves" to the rest of the world, and to their domestic populations. The more international obligations the nation has, the more vital is the process of sending messages that create desirable psychological responses in their recipients. As described in the previous section, the United States faces a sustained, multilevel Soviet PSYOP campaign. The campaign aims to discredit the United States and its allies in the view of the world and of their own populations.

Since mass communications became a PSYOP tool, the United States has been involved in several wars requiring domestic and international justification of its position versus adversaries such as the Germans, the Japanese, the Koreans and Chinese, and the Viet Cong. In each conflict, large-scale tactical PSYOP machinery also went into motion. Generally, such efforts have been a response to the initiative of an opponent; neither strategic nor tactical PSYOP apparatus has been at adequate strength before the threat appeared. And since World War II, moral and bureaucratic questions have interfered with coordination of PSYOP programs. As the definition of the word "war" becomes less clear, domestic perceptions of military and political goals become more vulnerable to psychological targeting by adversaries. This was seen most dramatically in Vietnam, but it also applies to current low-intensity conflict situations.

In World War II, a very effective PSYOP weapon of the United States was the charismatic leadership of Franklin Roosevelt, whose inspirational radio broadcasts were admired by Joseph Goebbels, Hitler's propaganda chief.[28] The United States created two major agencies for PSYOP activities in the war: the Office of War Information (OWI, for domestic and foreign propaganda), and the Office of Strategic Services (OSS, among whose functions was direction of military PSYOP). The OWI consolidated a number of information agencies that existed before the war. Wartime urgency did not prevent friction between the two agencies, congressional interference, and diffusion of PSYOP and propaganda decisionmaking among theater commanders of the Army and Navy--factors that hindered PSYOP missions in many cases.[29] But the propaganda of the OWI was marked by careful evaluation of target psychology, appropriate messages, and effective delivery. For example, the OWI aimed surrender appeals at the psychological vulnerabilities of fanatical Japanese soldiers, inducing large numbers to surrender in spite of a military code that seemingly precluded such behavior.[30] Although the United States PSYOP effort in World War II was somewhat cumbersome and disorganized, there were enough instances of such astute targeting to overcome the head start that the Axis powers had gained in propaganda.[31]

After the war, the word "propaganda" was associated in the United States with Fascism and Communism, the systems that had "reinvented" the device for their ideological advancement. The American public did not consider propaganda an activity to be pursued in peacetime by the leader of the free world. There followed a period of indecision about the role of PSYOP in peacetime, and most wartime PSYOP units were disbanded shortly after the war ended. When the Korean War began, only one operational psychological warfare troop unit existed. As in the previous war, a strong PSYOP effort was eventually mounted in Korea, offering mainly radio, loudspeaker, and leaflet support of conventional ground troops. But complaints of weak support often came from the PSYOP units at the front.[32] The Korean War was the stimulus for formation in 1951 of the Office of the Chief of Psychological Warfare (the first centralized agency for PSYOP) and the Psychological Warfare Center at Fort Bragg in l952. The former no longer exists, but the latter is now the center of PSYOP training and research for all the Armed Forces. In 1953 the United States Information Agency (USIA) was created for international dissemination of information.

In general, withdrawal from PSYOP activity after World War II was slowed by the realization that the Soviet Union was now a formidable enemy in the Cold War. This realization was based on two ideas: that the world does not automatically understand or approve of the United States; and that the Soviet Union is ready and able to exploit doubts about the morality and motives of the United States, in numerous overt and covert ways. An initial reaction to this situation was creation of the Central Intelligence Agency in l946, with authority for covert psychological and political activities. The size and scope of this organization grew very fast during the Korean War.[33]

Beginning about 1960, Communist expansionist doctrine has sought to exploit "wars of liberation" and insurgencies in areas previously under European colonial control. Soviet propaganda has portrayed the Soviet Union as defender of oppressed peoples, and the United States as an exploiting imperialist.[34] To meet this potent psychological gambit of guerrilla war, U.S. PSYOP applications in influencing the Third World and conducting unconventional warfare have become increasingly important in recent years.

How successful has the United States been in meeting postwar PSYOP challenges? The record has been mixed. A number of systemic differences prevent United States PSYOP from ever being the all-pervasive, centralized extension of foreign policy that it is for the Soviet Union. In the United States, all information cannot be officially controlled; secrecy is difficult even in the most critical cases; and decisionmaking always involves a number of conflicting views. The Soviet Ministry of Foreign Affairs is mobilized for propaganda activities that the United States State Department could never undertake. Likewise, no American institution has the total control exercised by the Communist Party of the Soviet Union.

The Vietnam War was the most recent large-scale PSYOP campaign of the United States. As in Korea, the main tactical devices were loudspeakers, leaflets, and radio. The Chien-Hoi (Open Arms) amnesty program stressed the strength of the South Vietnamese Army and the hopelessness of the Viet Cong position. In many respects, this massive effort fell short on both strategic and tactical levels: the first when domestic and international doubts about legitimacy were not met by United States official information, the second when PSYOP and military operations failed to complement each other, and the enemy was able to exploit the psychological vulnerabilities of both United States troops and the indigenous population of Vietnam.

However, a number of post-Korea United States psychological operations have been successful. In l965, American troops invaded the Dominican Republic to quell what was believed to be the first stage of a Castro-type revolution. During the American presence, liaison between military and civilian PSYOP groups was quite successful in supporting the military and political aims of the occupation.[35] According to verbal reports of participants, leaflets became such a valuable source of information that they were eagerly purchased in the capital city of Santo Domingo. In the Vietnam War, the Civilian Operations and Revolutionary

Development Support centralized and focused counterinsurgency targeting of indigenous populations in some areas.[36] The Joint U.S. Public Affairs Office (JUSPAO), founded to integrate public information and PSYOP functions in Vietnam, achieved a number of successes. CounterPSYOPs activity in Europe in the early 1980s ensured timely installation of intermediate-range missiles, despite an intensive Soviet psychological campaign to exploit European peace and antinuclear groups. And in the Grenada invasion of 1983, U.S. amnesty messages and rewards substantially reduced the opposing force.

After Vietnam, overall budgetary support for PSYOP declined. Army PSYOP units in Okinawa, Panama, and Germany were disbanded. This left the 4th Psychological Operations Group (consisting of four battalions in l988) at Ft. Bragg as the only active-duty unit in the United States Armed Forces with an exclusively PSYOP mission.[37] A National Guard unit remained in the Air Force and support units remained in the Navy, but Ft. Bragg became the source of PSYOP support for all types of military operations. If medium- and high-intensity conflict should break out, support would come from a reserve PSYOP unit trained at Ft. Bragg. In peacetime, the active-duty unit builds the research base for future readiness, and it has the mission of PSYOP support for low-intensity conflicts and peacetime overt activities.[38] Because the latter type of support has growing potential for application, a number of leading PSYOP authorities have agreed that United States capability needs to be expanded, and that PSYOP expertise should be integrated into standard U.S. military training. This group includes Alfred Paddock, formerly commander of the 4th Psychological Operations Group and director of psychological operations in the Pentagon; Melvin Kriesel and Michael Totten, former commanders of the 4th Psychological Operations Group; and Sam Sarkesian, professor of political science and former chairman of the Inter-University Seminar on Armed Forces and Society.[39]

Since the Reagan Administration put additional emphasis on information as one of the elements of national power, overt psychological operations in peacetime have been increased. These psychological operations have included training and advice to indigenous forces allied with the United States, surveys and assessments leading to actual operations, miscellaneous support to host nation PSYOP programs, and other overt PSYOP projects. Typical of PSYOP support to host nation programs is the long-term program created for El Salvador. One trainer is assigned to the U.S. military group in the capital, San Salvador, to coordinate all U.S. PSYOP programs in the country. Over the years the U.S. PSYOP contribution has resulted in significant change not only in the PSYOP practices of the El Salvadoran Armed Forces, but also in their general approach to insurgency, including an increased respect for human rights.

Programs similar to the El Salvadoran project exist worldwide, as established by DoD Directive S-3321.1. This directive requires every Unified and Specified Commander-in-Chief to conduct overt psychological operations in peacetime as appropriate to the military mission.

Overt psychological operations are coordinated with the State Department and require Country Team approval for each operation. The operations are coordinated with the United States Information Agency (USIA) to prevent dissemination of conflicting information. DoD operations attempt to fill the informational niches not filled by other agencies, dealing with subjects and areas of primary DoD concern but of secondary importance to the other information agencies.

At the strategic level, covert psychological activities are centralized in the Central Intelligence Agency, the latitude of whose operations has varied with the degree of oversight exercised by Congress. Meanwhile, overt propaganda is less centralized, and it is isolated from covert activity. In the l980s, the United States has sought to bolster programs of cultural relations and positive image-making abroad. "Public diplomacy" has been used much more aggressively to correct the record about United States intentions and in counterattacking Soviet and Cuban propaganda. In l983 a Special Planning Group was formed, including representatives from all government agencies having propaganda functions. The goal of this group was to centralize the public diplomacy effort and put forth a coherent, positive international image. The USIA has been instrumental in several specific improvements: coordinating United States explanations of Central American policy; ensuring INF installation in Europe; and increasing the budget for cultural relations and propaganda.[40] An interagency committee for public diplomacy, first used in the INF European campaign, continues low-key, behind-the-scenes coordination of policy statements and explanations.

But policy agencies still lack coordination with public diplomacy efforts; agency roles in PSYOP are not well defined; and the United States has often found itself in a reactive position in international situations requiring PSYOP applications. Because of agency compartmentalization, messages often lack the crucial element of credibility because they are contradictory. And, in the words of Army intelligence officer and scholar John Oseth, there is an "American suspicion of the tools of psychological manipulation,"[41] which insulates American institutions from association with such activities. On the military side, this takes the form of suspicion toward peacetime support of elite, special-purpose groups, such as those that would be given exclusively PSYOP missions.

A number of separate United States agencies now disseminate propaganda worldwide. The United States Information Agency runs the Voice of America and various cultural and information programs abroad. The Board for International Broadcasting runs Radio Free Europe and Radio Liberty, which broadcast into the Soviet bloc. And the Central Intelligence Agency continues its administration of covert PSYOP and counterPSYOPs activities abroad. DoD peacetime overt PSYOP activities have joined these groups in disseminating international information. Like the USIA, DoD disseminates international information only to foreign groups overseas.

As a result of governmental recognition of PSYOP deficiencies, in 1985 the Secretary of Defense promulgated a Master Plan to revitalize PSYOP. This plan reviewed the considerable inadequacies of PSYOP at that time, and recommended remedies for each item. Responsibility for DoD policy was given to the Under Secretary of Defense for Policy, which in turn created a Directorate for Psychological Operations assigned to the Deputy Under Secretary for Policy. This directorate was to be responsible for PSYOP policy and monitor response to the Master Plan.

The active duty PSYOP group was fully manned for the first time in years, and modernized equipment of all types replaced the Korean War-vintage radios, presses, and loudspeakers of the PSYOP units. PSYOP education and training were greatly improved, with a new Army functional area code assigned for PSYOP officers, and an enlisted military specialty was created. New awareness and staff training courses were created, to provide officers and enlisted personnel to meet a new demand for competent staff personnel. PSYOP staffs at all levels were created and strengthened, and they were moved out from under control of special operations staffs. The PSYOP Worldwatch Program was created, as a new, proactive body at the Joint Staff level, monitoring daily intelligence and open-source traffic for situations in which PSYOP input is appropriate. Similar bodies were created at the Unified and Specified Commands, adding a new element of proactive PSYOP to replace the traditional U.S. reactive posture. The Secretary of Defense assigned PSYOP forces to the newly created United States Special Operations Command, giving a four-star proponent for PSYOP and establishing a new support structure for Unified and Specified Command psychological operations across the spectrum of conflict. Heightened preparedness for wartime, contingency situations, low-intensity conflict, and peacetime operations resulted from the changes initiated from the Master Plan. By 1989, the response to the Master Plan had so changed the PSYOP environment that a new plan, was needed to accommodate the progress made since 1985. Because of the nature of PSYOP, these peacetime programs provide the most realistic training for PSYOP personnel. The overall effect of this PSYOP renaissance has not yet been calculated, but many successes in peacetime and low-intensity conflict have already been ascribed to it.

In conclusion, the United States has practiced psychological operations in the twentieth century when such measures were a military or diplomatic necessity, but there has been great reluctance to organize and maintain units with PSYOP capability during peacetime. When the "rules of the game" changed after World War II, awareness of the value of PSYOP gradually increased, and a number of organizations were given distinct functions such as covert activities and distribution of cultural information. But no overall, permanent coordination structure has appeared to maximize the PSYOP potential of each organization as needed, either on the tactical-military or the strategic-international level.

On the tactical level, United States military PSYOP staffing has been low, and military personnel are not widely trained in the goals and methods of psychological operations. Writers commenting on this situation have pointed out that the potential requirement of United States PSYOP aid to counterinsurgency in the Third World seems to be increasing, without appropriate improvement in readiness. Although efforts were made periodically toward a comprehensive U.S. tactical PSYOP doctrine, the policy has been to approach each case individually after it arises, with no overall philosophical context.[42] The most recent of those efforts, the DoD Master Plan, has focused greater attention and resources on the subject.

5. CONCLUSIONS

The time-honored principles of PSYOP retain exactly the same basic value as they have always had: as a force multiplier that complements military operations by lessening the determination of the target to resist. But since the days of Genghis Khan the definition of PSYOP has come to include a much broader range of activities and methods: from organized campaigns using leaflets and speakers in conventional tactical combat, to official statements by national leaders aimed at an international audience, to the everyday interaction of non-specialized military personnel with a host population. In spite of expanded application, the basic principles still apply: the message must be credible, meaning that it must be based in truth; it must be chosen and shaped to create a positive impression on the target audience; and it must be integrated into the overall military or political program of which it is part.

Contemporary PSYOP is practiced by many countries and agencies, in many circumstances, for a variety of goals. For the Soviet Union, it is a standard part of foreign policy, an accepted method of achieving national goals. For the U.S. it retains a negative connotation, both in political and military usage, although its utility has been proven in many situations. Consistency and coordination have been missing even in U.S. wartime PSYOP. For other nations involved in low-intensity or unconventional warfare as sponsors or participants, PSYOP has become an invaluable tool in gaining the support of segments of a population. For this reason, U.S. PSYOP support of allied nations, and effective

PSYOP approaches to neutral nations, has become a vital part of the U.S. program of protecting or influencing those countries.

All of this occurs in a world where: the chief potential military opponent has a dynamic, sophisticated, multilevel PSYOP apparatus; conventional military operations are increasingly costly, while PSYOP remains relatively inexpensive; and the shadow of nuclear war puts most world conflicts into vague, quasimilitary forms. Under these conditions the psychology of conflict assumes a primary role, one that must be understood by every military commander.

ENDNOTES

1. Fred W. Walker, "Truth Is the Best Propaganda: A Study in Military Psychological Operations." National Guard, October 1987, p. 27.

2. American Institutes for Research in the Behavioral Sciences, The Art and Science of Psychological Operations: Case Studies of Military Applications, vol. 1. (Washington: Department of the Army, 1976), p. 17.

3. United States Joint Chiefs of Staff. Dictionary of Military and Associated Terms. (Washington: GPO, 1984), p. 293.

4. United States Department of State. Contemporary Soviet Propaganda and Disinformation--A Conference Report. (Washington: Department of State, 1987), p. iii.

5. United States Congress, 97th. 2d Session. House. Permanent Select Committee on Intelligence. "Soviet Active Measures." Hearings, July l982, p. 32.

6. Oliver Thomson. Mass Persuasion in History. (Edinburgh: Paul Harris, l977), p. 3.

7. Jock Haswell. The Tangled Web--The Art of Tactical and Strategic Deception. (Wendover, England: J. Goodchild, 1975), p. 59.

8. Frank Barnett, B. Hugh Tovar, and Richard H. Shultz, eds. Special Operations in United States Strategy. (Washington: National Defense University Press, 1984), p. 20.

9. The Art and Science of Psychological Operations, p. 5.

10. Haswell, pp. 9-20.

11. Linebarger, pp. 14-16.

12. Linebarger, p. 21.

13. James M. Read, Atrocity Propaganda 1914-1919. (New Haven: Yale University Press, 1941), p. 159.

14. Linebarger, p. 81.

15. Chapman Pincher, The Secret Offensive. (New York: St. Martin's Press, 1985), p. 2.

16. D.A. Volkogonov, The Psychological War. (Moscow: Progress, 1986), p. 37.

17. United States Congress, pp. 34-35.

18. Bill Keller, "Moscow's Other Mastermind." New York Times Magazine, February 19, 1989, pp. 31-33.

19. Fred W. Walker, "Recent Changes in the Soviet Propaganda Machine." Journal of Defense and Diplomacy, May l988, pp. 47-50.

20. United States Congress, pp. 31-35.

21. United States Congress, pp. 39-43.

22. United States Congress, p. 87.

23. United States Congress, p. 170.

24. Pincher, pp. 60-61.

25. David Hertzberg, "Soviet Sponsored Clandestine Radio," in Joseph S. Gordon, ed., Psychological Operations--The Soviet Challenge. (Boulder, Colorado: Westview Press, l988), pp. 67-69.

26. Peter Kenez, "The Lesson of 007," in Gordon, pp. 77-85.

27. United States Information Agency. Committee to Oppose Soviet Active Measures. Soviet Active Measures in the Era of Glasnost: Prepared at the request of the U.S. House of Representatives, Committee on Appropriations. Washington, DC: USIA, 1988.

28. United States Congress, p. 49.

29. Charles Roetter, The Art of Psychological Warfare 1914-1945. (New York: Stein and Day, 1974), p. 128.

30. Roetter, pp. 130-131.

31. Roetter, pp. 136-137.

32. Linebarger, pp. 93-98.

33. Alfred H. Paddock, Jr., U.S. Army Special Warfare--Its Origins. (Washington: National Defense University Press, 1982), p. 100.

34. Paddock, p. 41.

35. Maurice A.J. Tugwell, "Soviet Propaganda in the Third World," in Gordon, p. 47.

36. Ron D. McLaurin, ed., Military Propaganda: Psychological Warfare and Operations. (New York: Praeger, 1982), pp. 282-285.

37. Barnett, Tovar, and Shultz, pp. 218-219.

38. Barnett, Tovar, and Shultz, p. 237.

39. Alfred H. Paddock, "Military Psychological Operations and U.S. Strategy," in Gordon, pp. 145-164; Michael W. Totten, "U.S. Army Psychological Operations and the Army Reserve," in Gordon, pp. 188-209; and Sam C. Sarkesian, "Organizational Strategy and Low Intensity Conflicts, in Barnett, Tovar, and Shultz, pp. 261-289.

40. Paddock, in Gordon, pp. 146-148.

41. John M. Oseth, "Public Diplomacy and US Foreign Policy," in Gordon, p. 139.

42. Joseph Miranda. "Political Warfare: Can the West Survive?" Journal of Social, Political and Economic Studies, Spring 1985, p. 7.

www.ingramcontent.com/pod-product-compliance
Lightning Source LLC
LaVergne TN
LVHW081321060426
835509LV00015B/1631
* 9 7 8 1 6 0 8 8 8 3 0 2 8 *